Judder Men
Ben Bransfield

smith|doorstop

the poetry business

Published 2021 by
Smith|Doorstop Books
The Poetry Business
Campo House,
54 Campo Lane,
Sheffield S1 2EG

Copyright © Ben Bransfield 2021
All Rights Reserved

ISBN 978-1-912196-54-8
Typeset by The Poetry Business
Printed by Biddles, Sheffield

Smith|Doorstop Books are a member of Inpress:
www.inpressbooks.co.uk

Distributed by NBN International, 1 Deltic Avenue,
Rooksley, Milton Keynes MK13 8LD

The Poetry Business gratefully acknowledges the support of
Arts Council England.

Contents

- 7 Go-Kart
- 8 Uncle David
- 9 The Twangers
- 10 Nan and Granddad's
- 11 Joe
- 12 Blundellsands
- 13 The Afterlife
- 14 Elizabeth Crescent
- 16 Powder Closet
- 17 Ann Salt, 30, and Martha Moors, 51, imprisoned six months for stealing a shirt. January 31, 1825.
- 18 A Rag Man
- 19 In his Garden
- 20 October
- 21 Refresher Course
- 22 Benicàssim
- 23 To King Ferdinand III of Castile, upon entering the Mezquita of Córdoba, 1236.
- 24 Tomatoes
- 26 Former Tenant
- 27 Delivery
- 28 Dogs dream
- 29 Lamprey
- 30 Bread
- 31 Paros

Notes

*for my family,
with love*

Go-Kart

We flew through our youth on its bolted back
of scrap wood and salvaged pushchair wheels,
tacked carpet tiles. Slow in that secret shed,
his workbench clamped the parts that met other parts
to bear a grandson's weight. We pulled the thing
like a dog on a lead up Cockshutt Lane to the Birch
where the see-saw and roundabout wanted our touch,
where the rusting rocket rocker that we'd climb astride
got no more than a look. Here for free fall, for the fast air,
to test what had been built, unable to think beyond
the setting off. To go faster we had to share, to bolt together,
to sit between each other's legs and quicken down there,
pull both strings taut lean back as one and steer.

Uncle David

At Southport Pleasureland,
the apple of the Caterpillar ride
behind your grey puffer jacket.

I was no longer six or seven
but there you were, tiptoeing,
beaming at the Big Dipper,
screamers who would survive.

You, about to take my hand,
and carry the fish I had won
with your help for a short while.

The Twangers

Tight brass coils to stop child-thrown doors
hitting walls. When twanged by my father
by trick of thumb, he'd summon them.

And wherever rang that quivering call –
the bellies of beds, the backs of floors,
from deep within the fluid of the eye,

already there in brain or inner ear
at higher pitch that only I could hear –
those sidewise judder men would come.

Nan and Granddad's

Corned beef. Silverskin onion juice
sluiced from the jar onto mash.
The rhubarb boiled brown to mush
under crumble, a curl of ice cream.

Upstairs? No-one really knew.
I whispered between them in bed
the night my brother was born,
where stories were spun against sleep.

The garden tilted up to mystery
and things beginning: greenhouse,
the shed, not a trace of the nails
he'd think he'd stolen from work.

And the black pond never let on
it had taken the goldfishes' tongues,
dumb oracles who rose to tell
but took down their pills and forgot again.

There's Mum, turned six, tipping
that bottle of dandelion and burdock –
it should have been somewhere safer,
his unlabelled homemade vinegar.

Joe

Startling as his longbow arrows
and his pierced ear, some years ago
he built a café on a hat
and wore it all the way to school.

His, the only Christmas present
you'd never see coming. One year,
a sawdust tea chest full of tat
to make me laugh, a lucky dip.

Walking round his exhibition,
I thought of Mum who'd let us paint
a tree of hands up the kitchen wall,
and his early thing for triangles.

The funny turns had left him
by the time he got his chickens.
He taught children how to blow eggs,
to watch sponge rise behind hot glass.

Blundellsands

North of Liverpool, where pines must heed the call
and drop again upon their rough-hewn cores

to serve the land – from every bay window
mums bear, then drag these precious loads

up Crosby beach, dry branches docked
by bauble thread, stray tinsel strand.

Another Place – one hundred cast iron men
stare out to sea, await the reckoning of tides

and bracing on the shore behind in lines,
those dead and dune-defending Christmas trees.

The Afterlife

i.m. Roy Fisher 1930–2017

Following the riddle of his directions
with the body of his work
slung in the sack at my shoulder,
I took Roy Fisher for a walk.

On the opposite climb of the vale
where the gods had left it,
a navel opening, grown over
and steep and far to come by.

Taking the page I thought most capable,
I pushed him into earth
with tiger's tooth and iron hen
and hoped he'd take me with him

to the garage of the middle land,
where it's always Sunday morning
and a lady with good lungs
plays a silver-banded bassoon.

Elizabeth Crescent

And here also is God, his grotto of lights
    strung from gutters down the pebble-dash walls
His side of the semi; guardian of the Shropshire stars,
    our universe of Broseley Wood. In the beginning
the deep gloss was a teak veneer sideboard
    shouldering grails and reliquaries: here,
three kittens on a powder blue collector's plate;
    behind the front fenders of a toy Rolls-Royce
with sidemount spare, a Merrythought bear; a stuffed parrot
    leaning into a Benthall sugar pot of earthenware;
perpetual calendar, still on November,
    and under domes of glass, two brass anniversary clocks
spinning from the first mover's touch.
    Mounted in corners, troves of spirits:
Captain Morgan keeping watch over
    the Malibu's coconut bulb, those hanging amber scotches
a mirage of optics full and twinkling
    above bottles of Dry and Babycham; Cherubim.

It's Christmas here too by the mounted gas fire,
    where painted Anaglypta bricks hide
behind cards on the bunting that rise and dip.
    This galaxy of Artex, this lampshade forgotten
under golden weeds of tinsel,
    waits out the siege of the red bows.
And Mr Garbett, lost in some chord at his electric organ;
    if he stops playing, the world will stop spinning
like this lit Dutch windmill, turning
    on a ledge where faded floral curtains part.
There, my little brother, further off,

  his fingers finding themselves for the first time
then it's on our way into silent night
  bearing paper bags fat with Midget Gems and Dolly Mixtures
that we'd send into orbit on ribboned Christingles,
  the little orange worlds we cupped in nervous palms,
trying not to spill the fuel eternal
  as wax wept its way down our still burning candles.

Powder Closet

Southside House, Wimbledon

Behind the tapestries, shut
in that cupboard of arsenic

pomade and lice, a boy
waits for horsehair perukes

and suet-greased wigs
to tilt back and dust.

No cone to protect his eyes,
his flourpuff lung.

What word does he whisper
to let them know it is done?

At what hour can he creep
back to the farm, white as a sheet?

Ann Salt, 30, and Martha Moors, 51, imprisoned six months for stealing a shirt. January 31, 1825.

We both had loved him once, despite the years
of slow pains and sudden births.

He'd watch us raise each brace of pheasant
from his belt, to hang for flavour.

When I plated lamb for him with steadied hands,
he called me his little finch.

She lost an eye the time he clapped her with his book –
like a hot egg dropped, the world spun.

And, knowing that sprats and dogs had better lots,
we still leapt at early suppers, danced for years on our knees.

She found him in the bath but didn't cry
and when they came I didn't hide his keepsake list.

It was the shirt he'd had us in – that we had split,
to keep it from our daughters' masters – that did us in.

A Rag Man

In the mist, a van appears
mister van peers in the app

mist in the ears, papa van
mist in the ears, a pavane

a pair vanish in the mist
a man peers in the vista

a mist appears in the van
ears in the van: a man sip it

is it vain the man spares
the man's spare visa in it?

ears in the van: aim an' spit
the man spears in a visit

ears in the van: a pain mist
ears in the van: a stain map

peer in the van, a name pissed
peer in the van, a pained mess

peer in the van, pansies made
hear me pant, vanish

In his Garden

I could see the red engine of the miniature train
glistening from the morning's lawn sprinklers.
On a wrought-iron table, a tiger cub was dozing.

Three manned gates beyond an open patio door,
where a curtain billowed out. The face already white
and tinted lenses darkening his brow.

I saw him glide back to the island in his second kitchen,
and crack an egg into a crystal highball tumbler. I watched
the bob of his Adam's apple as he drank it down.

October

Housemaster and boarders have gone home.
The gravel drive has let loose its stubble
and the pond is up to the sedge, the rugby boot.

The monument on Lilleshall Hill
wet, even from here, as the hoover
behind in Longford Hall sucks the life
out of the carpet, rattles down a toenail.

Everybody's pagan for a week.
Chimney after chimney offers up
its conclave for the Witch King to read.

Refresher Course

The leading blokes are fire fighters,
have seen it all. We tick off mouth to mouth,
asthma, the dummy-proof defibrillator.

The Head of Games gives himself up
to the recovery position – perpendicular knee,
arms that can't let him swallow his tongue.

This is what we must prepare to do.
Round come the practice EpiPens
we must punch into thighs and hold

for *four, five, six*. Tales of teachers
stabbing their own legs, surprising
their own thumbs with needles.

The Bursar is about to drop.
Your first response is crucial.

Benicàssim

The music kept us going into sunrise.
Bog-eyed on booze in greenhouse tents
our hanging temples drew us out. Penitent
revellers. We limped across flints and scree

like any shot and throbbing mountain deer
towards the showers. We washed away
cakes of blood, the slicks of someone's suncream.
Cleaned ourselves out for God one last time.

To King Ferdinand III of Castile, upon entering the Mezquita of Córdoba, 1236.

I am here. I am holding you up in your many places.
As I have always been, crutch and brace, I am again.
I am no different to before. Fire and earth and fire.

I am keystone, tesseræ, split and join. Arch after arch
you will roam for me, will deny more than five of my pillars
as I lift the mirage of empire, hold this desert tent and sky.

Bare your weary soles, *conquistador*. I will be jasper
brick and stone, whatever you let them do to me,
whichever way you face to pray.

Tomatoes

They come back to us, the dead, bearing fruit.
Pulling out weeds from the patio's cracks,
I left one greener finger there that had pushed
on through, as I struggled to mow the lawn,
as all else turned to scotch and died.
Without a drop it survived, and day by day
elbowed it out across the paving slabs,
sprouting shoots then leaves from nimble joints.
When the first yellow flower flared, I knew
he was there, and the bloods that would follow –
smooth green balls that would swell and fill
on those little vines, each bearing a dozen disciples.
I watched from the kitchen door, nervous that birds
wouldn't leave him alone or let his apology grow.
At dusk I gave him mist from our uncoiled hose,
pinched purple sprigs from the splits in his arms
to send earth's dark goods back down the shaft
so the fruits could crimson. Under a blood moon,
one night I dreamed I was marooned in him,
the house a jungle of vines and gas and heady oils,
where knobble-knot branches raised me
as one of their own, furring my garden tongue.
I fed from the warmest bombs, filled on the bang
of juice and seed and all that is tomato. And they
were greatly fleshed, and I went beneath the skin –
never to know hunger again in the gorge
and bank of them. I was Mowgli of the mandrakes,
and I clambered through the rest of him for days
to find the root and end of it all, where the codes
of the nightshade hid, where the *solanine tomatine*

toxins lay, safe in low dose, in their subtle supply.
Green with powder and spore, lingering lungfuls
of him inside me and finally freed from language.
Not a thorn or a slug between us. What an Eden
was there, what a greenhouse of atoms, each limb
fused to another, each tomato part of the answer –
a gift of life from my grandfather's second body
for the sun to ripen, for the gardeners' Mass
to be given, to be taken and broken open.

Former Tenant

I thought of him, dead in the pub and carried
back through the door our sofa wouldn't fit –
the triple distilled peat of his fogged flesh.

I still don't know his name, and post, not ours
is never his – but at the table in my sober hour,
alone, not even having to hear myself think,

I feel him there beside the purring fridge,
and it's not unkind – the way he combusts
like flour, over our landlord's chilling tiles.

Out the back on the postage stamp lawn,
someone's cat sizes us up, leaves its mark.
We pay for what cannot be owned.

Delivery

Last night I dreamed I pushed you out of me.
It didn't seem so strange. You weren't stillborn
this time, there was no cord about your neck,
no stoppered scream. There were no genes in you
but mine, and so, because it was a simple cure –
to halt the self-destruct that would be free
in you too soon, before you came of age –
they made me put out eyes that I had grown
from seed, then watch our red penance break
like waters from my knackered hairy knees.
I woke then peed a spurt in starts, where you
had been, where I had turned into that tree,
and wept to know you could not, would not, be.

Dogs dream

that we will butt out and leave them to it
  under parked wagons in the rain,
  rutting like wolves on the bare arse of Primrose Hill.

that the amygdala is the seat of the soul,
  that dead lovers ride on night barks
  long knackered by fox shit runs.

that inverted words on a calculator screen
  or the paperclip reset of a Tamagotchi
  is only the beginning.

that they die a small death every night,
  that they catch up with what they were
  before we came with our extendable leads.

Lamprey

Some mornings, I remind myself I am not a lamprey.
It's not acceptable to sludge along the river's bed
like a severed penis or an unfried length of black pudding,
unfurling in a trance, in a clench of razor teeth.
Though I'll not face the glut of kings as they do,
I too have known the Balrog of the leeches,
silting what the water dumps of blood and flesh.
Thrift-demon, we are dead end. We are both a one-way trap.
One night I might deflate down the plughole
boneless, nothing more than muscle memory.
With spermicidal focus, I'll come whipping quietly
upstream for the moonlit skinny dippers.

Bread

For five thousand years, men have mixed flour and water,
have led each other deep into golden fields of spelt
where wind-stroked heads part like thought from word,
keeping watch above husks of rye while the wild yeast forms.
It has done us no harm, to learn what is bread
and butter, to taste what must spoil in time and harden.
After the milling, you are all that is left – a split coat of seed.
What is good has to give, has to stretch under heel of the palm
and the punch down that comes leaves a bruise that is hidden,
the baker's shame. Yet, over tempered flame before the dawn
in pits of blackened clay, in griddle pan and iron stove, we rise.
At our own good tables we will take what crust must be broken,
as body into frail body, as salt into steam. So much of the earth
rests in each leavened loaf. Forgive us. We know what we know.

Paros

There again, the only family at the open air taverna
somewhere high off the road down to Naoussa.
It's as lovely as before, to sit and watch you relax,
enjoying that plate of good and simple food –
chicken souvlaki, the island cheese in the salad
softer than feta and alive with raw onion, oregano.
A carafe of chilled red wine on the wooden table,
split Parian figs in a bowl on the whitewashed hatch.

Going back for a closer look, those young French owners
I'm sure you thought were sisters,
who welcomed us over to their cool quiet patio
in the cicada-whirring early evening hours,
will come out from the kitchen with a basket of bread
for us and a plate of chips for Joe, kind and at ease
and just as in love as before. We will pour what's left
into our empty glasses. Mum will look out towards the sea.

Notes

The sentencing of Ann Salt and Martha Moors 'for stealing a shirt' was reported in *The Manchester Guardian* on January 31, 1825 and is drawn from the *Guardian* digital archive record, 'Seven Years for a Pound of Butter'.

Antony Gormley, *Another Place*, 1997. Cast iron 100 elements / 189 x 53 x 23 cm. Crosby Beach, Liverpool.

'The Afterlife' is both in memory of Roy Fisher and uses words from his poem of the same title in *Standard Midland* (Bloodaxe, 2010).

Acknowledgements

Thanks are due to the editors of the following publications, in which some of these poems first appeared: *The Interpreter's House, Magma, The North, Orbis, Oxford Poetry, Poetry Ireland Review, Poetry Salzburg Review, Poetry Wales, Stand*, and *Under the Radar*. Thanks especially to Jane Commane, Jacob Sam-La Rose, and the Poetry School for their mentoring through *Primers: Volume Two* (Nine Arches Press), where 'Delivery' was first published.

Heartfelt thanks go, firstly, to Peter Sansom for his editorial guidance and generosity, and to Katie and The Poetry Business team. Warm thanks to the following people for encouragement and early feedback on some of these poems: John-Paul Burns, Harry Chapman, Adam Cross, Sasha Dugdale, Keith Hutson, Michael Laskey, Helena Nelson, Richard Scott, Jean Tuomey, and Rod Vincent.

I am thankful to all at the Arvon Foundation, Tŷ Newydd, and especially grateful for residencies at The Tyrone Guthrie Centre at Annaghmakerrig.

Special thanks, as always, to Ann Sansom and Peter Carpenter for their continued support and belief in my writing.